W9-BGU-577

REFLECTIONS OF BLUE
A PICTORIAL HISTORY OF THE U.S. NAVY BLUE ANGELS
By CAROL KNOTTS

Copyright © 1979 by SK Publications, Bossier City, Louisiana.
All rights reserved. Printed in the United States of America.

Art Direction by Vickie M. Graham
Typography by Vitro Press/Fort Walton Beach, Florida

ISBN: 0-933424-24-8
Library of Congress catalog card number: 80-52624

First Edition October 1979
Second Edition October 1980

Specialty Press

Box 426
729 Prospect Avenue
Osceola, Wisconsin 54020

For Ted and Sally . . . .

FOREWORD

The Blue Angels have always held a special place in my heart. Looking heavenward as I watch their precise aerial maneuvers, I cannot help but think of the time when our ancestors first looked to the skies, fascinated by the mysteries of shooting stars and had visions of angels and winged gods.

Recently, this fascination was mingled with deep felt pride when the Blue Angels bestowed upon me the title of honorary commander of the team. As a Navy man from way back, I once again saw in this honor the highest traditions of the naval service.

The majesty of flight is something too many of us take for granted, especially in a world of commonplace technological growth. Watching the Blue Angels sweep by overhead in those impossible formations, I am reminded of the greatness of our achievements in the world of aviation. Today the Blue Angels carry on great traditions, serving to remind us not only of the accomplishments of the past, but of the hope and wonder apparent in our own future.

ERNEST BORGNINE
Honorary Commander/Leader

ACKNOWLEDGEMENTS

The pursuit of information and photographs covering more than three decades of Blue Angel history led down many paths. Some were short, within the confines of Pensacola or even Blue Angels' headquarters itself. Others ended several thousand miles away in such places as California and New York. Wherever the various paths took me, I am indebted to many individuals for their contributions.

The hours spent around the officers and enlisted personnel of the Blue Angels at El Centro and Pensacola were invaluable in learning the operational procedures of the squadron. It is impossible to name each team member individually but my special thanks is extended to all of them, especially Cmdr. Bill Newman, Lt. Kent Horne, Lt. Jack Ekl, Lt. Ray Sandelli, Lt. Jack Johnson, YN1 Bob White, DM1 Lou Humphery, PH1 John Porter and all of ''Fat Albert's'' flight crew. My personal thanks and appreciation goes to McDonnell Douglas tech rep Dale Specht for his unending support.

Much of the historical information and many of the earlier photos were contributed by these former Blue Angels: Ray Hawkins, Jim Barnitz, Bruce Bagwell, Scotty Ross, Bill Wheat, Zeke Cormier, Billy May, Casey Jones, Jack Reavis, Jack Dewenter, Ed Holley, Ken Wallace and Bob Aumack.

Other contributors of historical materials were Harry Gann of McDonnell Douglas, Bill Larkins, MSgt. (USAF) Robert Denham and Dave Scheuer, former Grumman tech rep with the Blues from 1951-1968 and only the second person recognized as an honorary commander/leader by the team.

I also appreciate the assistance of Herman J. Schonenberg, Lynn McDonald and Lois Lovisolo of the Grumman History Center, Bethpage, N.Y., and Bob Carlisle of the Naval Photographic Center, Washington, D.C.

A very special friend of the Blues, Trader Jon, shared many stories of the past seasons. His establishment in downtown Pensacola is a personal museum for Blues memorabilia and my thanks to him for the hours I spent sitting among his one-of-a-kind souvenirs.

Penny Matthews of Ft. Walton Beach spent hours typing and correcting the manuscript and I thank her for her expertise and enthusiasm.

A special and most lasting thanks to Mr. Ernest Borgnine for contributing the foreword. His long friendship with the team and his unique title as honorary commander/leader reflect the respect that completely different, but equally dedicated professionals, share for each other.

INTRODUCTION

Six o'clock in the morning is usually a quiet hour of the day along the NAS El Centro flight line. Night sky gives way to traces of mellow pinks which rapidly change to flaming oranges as the sun climbs above the flat, dark green lettuce fields of the Imperial Valley.

Men moving about the hard, grayish concrete are transformed from similar dark silhouettes to figures in deep blue uniforms and brown leather flight jackets. The center of their attention is six blue and gold A-4Fs. Aligned in a row, nose-high, the planes mirror the rising sun across dew-beaded, highly-polished wing and fuselage surfaces. Images of the other A-4Fs reflect from the silver bordered intakes and tapered blue bodies and wings. Other reflections catch the eye - an out

of focus #3 from the tail next in line or a helmet bag with a yellow polyurethane occupant hanging beneath a tapering jet snout.

Standing there it doesn't take much imagination for the sleek, stream-lined jets to become robust, thick-nosed planes of another era -- three prop blades, a hub front and a heavy looking, un-marked ink-blue cowling. No decal or bands of lighter color appear below the squared off canopy positioned almost midway along the plane's length. The canard wings extend outward from their attachment at the fuselage, well below, but directly beneath the single canopy.

Moving to the rear, the dark blue body narrows, distinguished only by a large U.S. NAVY marking. The last several feet sweep

upward forming a large, single tail. A white number stands out against the deep blue of the tail - so far the only resemblance to their sister ships of a jet age. The Hellcat rests on a "Tail Dragger" landing gear, its big blades facing skyward. No helmet bag hangs below the tilted nose. Leather flying caps and goggles are the flight attire of the F6F pilot.

Echoes of those earlier planes fade from the eye as the A-4Fs again appear in their true place in the surface reflections. But their memory will not fade ... for their presence echoes the beginning of the U.S. Navy Blue Angels flight demonstration team, nurtured and raised with pride and tradition into today's Blue Angel team ... recognized throughout the world for their aerial artistry.

EARLY CATS
The Pre-Korea Years of The F6F-5, F8F-1, F9F-2

The U.S. Navy's pride in its aviation division has deep roots, beginning with the early airships of Samuel Pierpoint Langley. From wood and cloth to the metal airframes of the 1920s and 30s, ideas were tested. World War II and aerial battles over the Pacific convinced any doubters that the future of Navy aviation was unlimited. Following the war, the idea of forming an official flight exhibition team to perform at air shows across the country for the purpose of Navy recruitment began to gain support at high levels.

On April 24, 1946, a directive from the Chief of Naval Operations called for the organization of a flight exhibition team. The base of choice was the Naval Air Station (NAS) Jacksonville in Jacksonville, Florida, and the man chosen to form the team was Lt. Cmdr. Roy "Butch" Voris, an experienced WW II pilot and combat training officer.

In less than two months, on June 15, 1946, the team flew its first public show at the Southeastern Air Show in Jacksonville. With no official name during their early days the team continued to expand their demonstrations to sites across the U.S.

A workhorse of the recent war, the Grumman F6F-5 Hellcat, had been selected as the team's demonstration aircraft. She was a tough and proud prop-engined fighter who had matured many a combat naval aviator. Powered by a Pratt & Whitney R2800-10W radial air-cooled engine, the three-bladed prop produced a thrust of 2,000 hp and allowed for a speed of more than 400 mph. Her 9,200 lbs were spread over a span of 42' 10", a length of 33' 7", and a height of 13 feet. The F6F could operate to a ceiling of 38,000 feet, but for the team's purpose her flight capabilities would always be displayed within the first few thousand feet of her natural element.

Originally assigned four F6Fs and a single SNJ, Voris designed the demonstrations around three aircraft flying a variety of loops and rolls in a wedge formation and a simu-lated "dogfight" using three F6Fs with the SNJ acting the part of a Japanese "Zero." The fourth F6F was used as a spare aircraft but within a short time had been elevated to the role of solo.

By late July the team had become known as the Lancers, but within a month a new name - Blue Angels - had replaced it. Legend credits a New York trip and an advertisement for the city's famous Blue Angel nightclub as the inspiration for their new name. It would be carried with honor by all the people selected to be a part of its history, not only through peacetime, but even during another war.

In August, 1946, a newer, faster machine was assigned to the Blue Angels, the F8F-1 Bearcat. Also manufactured by Grumman, she had a modified R2800 engine. However, unlike her predecessor, she had a four-bladed prop and produced a 2,100 hp thrust which allowed for speeds in excess of 450 mph. The Bearcat could fly above 40,000 feet. Slightly heavier at 9,600 lbs, she divided the weight over a span of 35' 6", a length of 28' 3", and a height of 13' 10".

By mid-1947 the changes in personnel, aircraft and procedures had produced an air show different from those of the first year. Lt. Cmdr. Robert Clarke now flew #1 and all four F8Fs were performing for the first time in a diamond formation.

January 1948 saw Lt. Cmdr. "Dusty" Rhodes installed as the new flight leader and before the year was out, the Blue Angel name would appear on the aircraft for the first time. In November the team was reassigned from NAS Jacksonville to NAS Corpus Christi, Texas. Continuing to thrill millions across the country with their close-formation, precision-timed maneuvers, the Bearcat pilots added show after show to their log book.

A major and lasting change occured in August 1949 as the F8Fs were replaced by the first jet aircraft assigned to the team. Various adjustments in the type, timing and sequence of maneuvers were required. With the introduction of the jet, the Blue Angels' association with the prop plane was over but never to be forgotten. The F6Fs and F8Fs had recorded more than 300 shows before some 12 million spectators. They had been - and would forever be - the heart of the growing and deepening Blue Angel spirit.

Though their association with propeller-driven aircraft was at an end, their relationship with Grumman was not. The new plane was the Grumman built F9F-2 Panther. She was a pilot's envy and a spectator's delight. A tricycle landing gear supported the Panther's sleek aerodynamic profile of sharp nose and narrow fuselage. Her straight wings displayed highly polished, leading edges and ended in tapered, fuel-carrying tip tanks. A British Rolls-Royce Nene engine producing 5,000 lbs of thrust, allowed the F9F-2 to reach speeds of 525 mph and operate at an altitude of some 44,600 feet. She weighed 9,300 lbs and had a span of 38 feet, a length of 40 feet, and a height of 15 feet. The Panther required special modifications for the team's purposes — certain adjustments in the hydraulic system and lateral control surfaces, new navigational devices, and a special paint scheme. The Blues introduced their new jets to the public for the first time at Beaumont, Texas, on August 20, 1949. Almost on the heels of the new jets came a new home as the team transferred to NAS Whiting Field near Pensacola, Florida, in late September.

Lt. Cmdr. Johnny Magda took over as the new Blue Angel leader in early 1950. Twenty-four demonstrations later, on July 30 at NAS Dallas, the team displayed their flying skills to the American public for the last time. The Korean War had started and Magda was being reassigned to a carrier and combat duty. All Blue Angels - both officers and enlisted men - volunteered to go with Magda. By August 1950 the Blue Angels had disbanded and the men reported to California for transition to combat status. They left behind a history of tradition and pride and a record of duty expertly done.

Between 1946 and 1950 the team had been viewed by more than 14 million people in some 380 demonstrations. It was a time the Blue Angels would never forget. It was a time the millions who had watched them would never forget. And most important of all, it was a time the Navy would never forget. . . .

July 4, 1946 - Contest entries poured in all week for the contest to name the Flight Exhibition Team, indicating widespread interest in the crack fliers who are giving the public a sample of the quality of flying taught in naval aviation.

Breaking all previous records of past contests, the Yard Mail was crammed full of all sorts of suggested names for the team. They ran the gamut from such mouthfuls as "The Flying Power of the PAC's" to such staccato ones as "Jaxcats," "Aero Aces," and the "Jaxateers." Some of the more colorful ones included:

"Com-Bats."
"Death-Cheaters."
"Sky-Jackers."
"The Flying Buccaneers."
"The Sea Eagles."
"Top Notchers."
"The Goshawks."
"The Blue Bachelors."
"The Sky Rocketeers."
"The Skyscrapers."
"The Cloud Busters."
"Navy Cats."
"Century Thunder Birds."
"Naval Cavaliers."
"Strat-O-Cats."
"Aerocats."

All entries will be judged on merit alone, it was pointed out, with the judges selecting the $10 winner without previous knowledge as to the name of the person submitting it. The contest will continue until a desirable designation is found for the team.

Rules for the contest are simple. Just send in the name you think most suitable on a piece of paper via Yard Mail. Be sure to include your full name, rank or rate, and department. Mail it to the Editor, JAX AIR NEWS, Box 2.

If this is any help -- it was reported this week that the team would definitely be equipped with F8F Bearcats in the near future.

A reprint of an article appearing in the July 4, 1946, issue of the Jax News. The contest never produced a name with which the team felt comfortable.

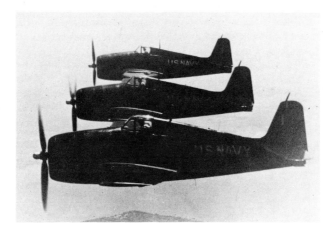

Eyeball to eyeball in a line-abreast formation during practice over Jacksonville.

The attire of the well-dressed Blue Angel is clearly evident in this 1946 photo of the first team: Lt. Al Taddeo, Lt. (jg) Gale Stouse, Lt. Cmdr. "Butch" Voris, Lt. Maurice Wickendoll, and Lt. Mel Cassidy. Actually, Lt. Taddeo had replaced another pilot, Lt. Cmdr. Lloyd Barnard, originally chosen by Voris but transferred to other naval duties before the team's first public air show.

Lt. Cmdr. Voris, Lt. Al Taddeo, and Lt. Wickendoll form the standard wedge formation of the first year. The F6F Hellcat served the team for only 13 air shows, its last public appearance being July 21 at Omaha, Nebraska's, World Fair of Aviation.

August 1946: Brand new F8F Bearcats at the Grumman factory in Bethpage, N.Y., join the team. At an air show on August 24 in Denver, the team would use the name Blue Angels for the first time.

Part of the 15-man maintenance crew assigned to the team the first year. From their dedication would come the long history and pride of no Blues' performance ever being cancelled due to mechanical problems.

Voris (second from the left) conducts a ramp preflight for Taddeo, Wickendoll, Cassidy and newest member Lt. (jg) Robby Robinson.

11

This close-up shot of Robinson's F8F shows good detail of the identity of pilot and crew chief on the canopy rail, the bubble canopy and the four-bladed prop. Robinson normally flew the solo position. He was the first Blue to die while on the team, the result of a crash during a show on September 29, 1946, at NAS Jacksonville.

Stilled props, folded wings and 2,100 horses wait for the next demonstration.

Folded-wing F6Fs form the background for their proud F8F relatives at Oakland, California.

Gear coming up, the wedge leaps into the air to begin another thrilling 20-minute show.

By mid-1947 the solo aircraft had evolved through a stage of taking part in the "Zero" demonstration to a full-fledged place in a new diamond formation. The first full diamond show was flown on June 7 at the World Air Carnival in Birmingham, Alabama.

Late 1947 shot of Lt. Bob Thelen, Lt. Chuck Knight, Lt. Cmdr. Bob Clarke, Lt. Cmdr. "Dusty" Rhodes (soon to assume command) and Lt. (jg) Billy May.

August 1948: British Sea Fury and Sea Hornet aircraft join the Blues at the dedication of Idlewild Field, N.Y. Both President Harry Truman and Governor Thomas Dewey were among thousands who watched the team during six days of ceremonies.

Tail numbers occur in an unusual sequence in this echelon photo. The pre-Korea pilots often flew interchangeable positions when necessity dictated, though on joining the team, each was assigned a specific position.

May 1949: Lt. George Hoskins and his crew chief AD1 D. R. Miller prepare for takeoff. People at the Denver air show were able to get a close-up view of the new paint scheme of yellow cowling name and wing leading edge.

The Blues' first patch was designed in May 1949. It soon appeared on the team members' uniforms but would not replace the cowling script name until a later date.

Traveling between distant show sites, the Bearcats got additional range from fuel in their external 150-gallon belly drop tanks.

Foothills near Fresno, California, frame the slot Bearcat as the team reaches the end of a cross-country flight.

An F8F stands next to her larger, swifter jet-age F9F-2 replacement on the ramp at NAS Corpus Christi. While transitioning to the F9F-2 Panther, shows continued in the Bearcat with the last prop F8F show flown on August 14, 1949 at Madison, Wisconsin.

Pilots' and crew chiefs' names are affixed on the fuselages of the new F9F-2s in mid-1949. Note the addition of the Blue Angel decal (now featuring jets) on the nose.

The team relaxes and waits for refueling to be completed before a practice session which will later be featured in a 1949 article in "Life" magazine.

Lt. Cmdr. Magda converses with Jake Swirbul, president of Grumman. Note the numbered left intake cover and the exposed 20 mm. nose cannon in the F9F-2s.

Practicing above the home waters of north Florida, the F9F-2s jocky into position for a left echelon roll. During 1949 and 1950 the jets would perform in 42 air shows.

The team that went to Korea: Lt. Jake Robcke, Lt. Pat Murphy, Lt. (jg) Fritz Roth, Lt. Cmdr. Johnny Magda, Lt. George Hoskins, and Lt. Ray Hawkins. Not pictured is Lt. Bob Belt, maintenance officer.

Following their last public show on July 30, 1950, the Blue Angels flew to California for reassignment to Korea as the nucleus of VF 191 on the U.S.S. Princeton. The officers and enlisted members of the team followed Cmdr. Magda into battle with the same dedication to duty as in the months of demonstration flying. During the combat months, formations were flown in F9F-5 Panthers and the pilots answered to the squadron name of "Satan's Kittens." Some who were their shipmates and aerial brothers would go forth to help reform an Angel team following Korea.

Holding a wing position over the Sea of Japan isn't much different than over the Gulf of Mexico.

Two of "Satan's Kittens" pass over the U.S.S. Princeton.

RETURN TO PEACEFUL SKIES

The F9F-5

Fourteen months after the Blue Angels were dissolved for the more needed duty of sorties in the skies over Korea, they were back home. The Navy, realizing the example of professionalism inherent in any Blue Angel performance, decided to reactivate their air demonstration team. Three of the men who had been a part of the 1950 team and three from the Pre-Korea years would become a part of the rebuilding. They were Lt. Ray Hawkins, Lt. Pat Murphy, Lt. Bob Belt, Lt. Frank Graham, and Lt. Mac MacKnight.

But tragic history had taken its toll. Johnny Magda would not return to the lead position. He had been shot down and killed during a mission in March 1951. A former Blue Angel, familiar to all, was called upon for lead duties a second time, "Butch" Voris.

Assigned to operate for a second time out of NAS Corpus Christi, the new team was given seven F9F-5 Panthers, two F7U-1 Cutlasses and one F8F Bearcat. The new Panthers were the same type aircraft the team had flown over Korea. They were a modification of the older F9F-2 with a more powerful Pratt & Whitney J-48-P-4 turbojet engine, an increased thrust to 6,250 lbs and a top speed of 625 mph. She was a plane capable of operating at altitudes above 50,000 ft and her weight of 10,147 lbs was well balanced over a span of 38 feet, a length of 42 feet, and a height of 16 feet.

With reactivation, the Navy redefined the team's mission from "representing the Navy at air shows and similar events" to "demonstrating precision techniques of naval aviation to naval personnel, and if directed, to the public."

Commander Voris and his squad practiced throughout the latter months of 1951 and early 1952. By mid-June they had become honed into a crisp, crack aerial unit and proved it on June 19, 1952, in their opening air show at the Memphis Mid-South Naval Festival. Welcomed by thousands of their former fans, the Blue Angels were back in business.

The 1953 season began with Cmdr. Voris replaced as leader by Lt. Cmdr. Ray Hawkins. As their Panthers looped and rolled their way through some 10 different diamond and echelon maneuvers, interspersed by dazzling solo passes, the winds of temporary change developed. A newer version of the F9F-5, called the F9F-6, had become a part of the Navy's aerial stock and the Blues made preparations for a mid-year shift to the newer version. Still flying shows in the Panther, the team made a trip to Grumman on Long Island to pick up their new planes.

However, during their August 4 return trip to Corpus Christi, problems in the #1 jet forced Lt. Cmdr. Hawkins to make a supersonic bailout. Investigations proving the immediate need for modifications to all F9F-6 aircraft resulted in the termination of any team plans for the new plane and a continued life for the F9F-5 as the "trademark" of the Blue Angels.

Following participation in a Cinerama production filmed during December and January of 1953-54, Ray Hawkins turned over command of the Blues in February to Lt. Cmdr. Zeke Cormier in the team's first aerial change-of-command ceremony. Another new tradition was begun as the first Marine pilot, Capt. Chuck Hiett, joined the team in 1954 to fly one of the wing positions.

The largest crowd ever, more than 54 million, viewed the team on nation-wide television in May 1954 on the Dave Garroway "Today" show.

As the 1954 season drew to a close with a December performance for the dedication of the U.S.S. Forrestal, so did the team's last association with their faithful Panthers. Since the rebirth of the team she had been the nucleus of more than 130 air shows, and though she would no longer fly the skies as a Blue Angel, she would always be a part of their history.

An incomplete Blue Angel F9F-5 stands on the line at NAS Corpus Christi in late 1951. Still to be added is the pilot's name under the canopy rail and the team decal on the nose. Note the polished front area of the wing tanks and the plugged nose gun ports which are in contrast to characteristics of the F9F-2.

Trailing red, white and blue smoke, the Blues pass through the clouds above Jacksonville, Florida.

Relaxing prior to a show at Detroit in August 1952.

One of the 25 support personnel assigned to the team makes a final check of the tail access cover.

At Glenview, Illinois, two of the support crew prepare the tip tanks with water. Weather forced a cancellation of the show later in the day.

Officers and enlisted team members work together to push Voris' plane back onto the concrete after it became stuck in softer grass and mud at Cleveland.

Cmdr. Voris and teammates Pat Murphy, Tom Jones, Ray Hawkins, Buddy Rich and Bud Wood pause between practice sessions at Corpus Christi.

A family portrait of the 1952 Blue Angels. Note that on the F9F-5s, the crew chiefs' names did not appear under the pilots' names.

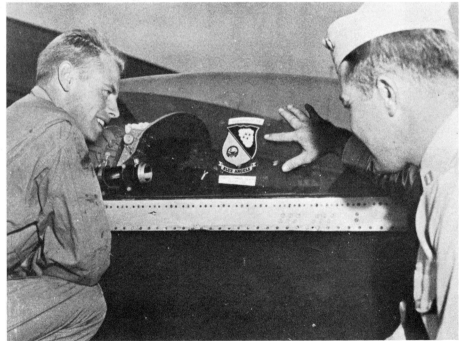

The "seal of approval." Team maintenance personnel often helped with needed repairs on any visiting aircraft -- but always left their mark by decorating it with a "repaired by the Blue Angels" decal.

Lt. Tom Jones putting the solo Panther through its paces at one of the 30 demonstrations during the 1952 season.

Shifting from a right echelon, the planes maneuver into position for the completion of the change-over roll.

A right echelon pass with speed brakes lowered at each air show gave any and all fans a good, long look at the Blues.

The highly polished metal of the wing root, wing leading edges and tip tanks stands out in this diamond shot.

The 1953 team: left to right: Lt. Mac MacKnight, Lt. Frank Jones, Lt. Pat Murphy, Lt. Cmdr. Ray Hawkins, Lt. Buddy Rich, (kneeling) Lt. Aus Aslund, Lt. Cmdr. Frank Graham and Grumman tech rep Dave Scheuer.

Four $500,000 jets roll into the sun high over the California landscape.

Practice makes perfect.

The diamond climbs above pastured farmland at a midwestern show site.

Red or blue food coloring added to the water in the tip tanks produced the colorful smoke trails. Note the Panther on the right sleeve.

A perfect alignment of the two wingmen is illustrated as the team poses at 300 mph for a PR photo.

With fans watching and waiting, the F9F-5s are moved into launch position preceding a demonstration in Illinois.

Lt. Cmdr. Hawkins and his traveling cohorts file a flight plan before deploying for another show site.

One of the F9F-6 "Cougars" lands at NAS Corpus Christi. It had just completed a six-ship flight from New York during which a horizontal stabilizer malfunction forced Lt. Cmdr. Hawkins to make a supersonic 750 mph ejection over Mississippi at an altitude of 35,000 feet. The ejection gave Hawkins the distinction of being the first man ever to survive a supersonic bailout. After he rejoined the team the following day, the Blues continued practices with the new aircraft for a short while. A recall of all F9F-6s to correct a flight control problem and the necessity of the aircraft for fleet operations, resulted in the team's never accepting the "Dash-Six" Cougar.

Never having flown a public show in the F9F-6, the Blues remained with their trusty F9F-5s until the end of the 1954 season.

Shadows chase the slow-moving Panthers as the team approaches a formation right echelon landing. Formation takeoffs had been a standard with the Blues since prop days but the formation landing began with the arrival of jets in 1949.

One of the most popular PR photos of the Panther era.

Lt. Bud Rich stands with Lt. Cmdr. Gus Brady and Lt. (jg) J. Barrow following their coast-to-coast record breaking three-hour and 45-minute flight on April 1, 1954. Lt. Rich had finished his tour with the Blue Angels some three months before and within less than two months would be killed in a catapult accident aboard the U.S.S. Bennington.

The Blues make a rolling pass within range of a photographer flying in an F2H-2P Banshee photojet.

Lettuce fields of the California central valley pass underneath the wings of the Navy's finest.

The pride of the men who flew the F9F-5s was matched only by the men who maintained the blue and gold chariots. Note the show uniforms worn by the support personnel.

Following 49 demonstrations during the 1953 season, the Blues spent part of the 1954 winter training period making a movie.

A right echelon roll was only one of some 10 four-ship maneuvers performed during the team's 25-minute show.

North Florida's pine forests and sandy soil slide beneath the Blue Angels' wings as they head home to Corpus Christi following a weekend of air shows.

COUGAR MAKES THE TEAM

The F9F-8

Sometimes a machine constructed from hands and ideas makes her aerial environment look like it was created for the machine instead of visa versa. Such a plane had evolved with the swept-winged sisters of the F9F-5s. The team had only a fleeting association with the earlier F9F-6, but with the F9F-8 version, the combination of Blue Angel pilots and Cougar aircraft made a beautiful and impressive match.

After the plane's arrival in January 1955, practice sessions took on a new look of symmetry and tightness which was unattainable in the former straight-wing aircraft.

On the ground or in the air, the sharp 35° swept-back line of the wings was clearly evident. Often referred to as the "Dash-Eight," the Cougar's roaring Pratt & Whitney P-48-P-8 turbo jet engine, producing 7,250 lbs of thrust, could push her through the air at transonic speeds of 700 mph and to heights of 42,000 ft. Tipping the scales at 11,865 lbs, she appeared deceptively light, almost dainty, as the weight was distributed over a span of 34' 6", a length of 41' 7", and a height of 12' 3".

Millions of old fans and thousands of new faces enjoyed the thrills of the newest member of the team. Lt. Cmdr. Cormier continued to lead the diamond and echelon through tight, graceful, wing-overlapped sequences, while the solo displayed his swept-winged steed's maximum performance capabilities in a series of rolling, climbing and runway-skimming maneuvers. Appearances on such popular television shows as "Navy Log" and the "Mickey Mouse Club" were additions to the team's busy schedule of performances scattered across the small towns, big cities, civilian sites and military bases of the country.

Mid-way through the 1955 season the unit said goodby to their adopted home at NAS Corpus Christi and followed orders reassigning them to NAS Pensacola in north Florida. The team's transfer was necessitated by the increased conditions of air congestion in the Corpus Christi area and the recent completion of a new jet facility at the Florida base. The Pensacola location was very near the Blues' former F9F-2 home, Whiting Field. Within their nine years of existence, the Blue Angels had now come to know four home bases. No one could forget the historic beginnings at NAS Jacksonville, the early jet days of Whiting Field or the two different eras of props and jets at NAS Corpus Christi. But the roots the team would put down at Pensacola would go the deepest and reach the farthest. From July 1955, every man or woman who wore the Blue Angel patch would call NAS Pensacola, "home."

In September 1956 the people of Canada got their first official look at the Blues. Two consecutive demonstrations in Toronto were viewed by more than 475,000 spectators and proved to be only the first in a series of future visits to Toronto and other Canadian showsites.

Cmdr. Cormier exchanged his Blue Angel patch and flight suit for a less exciting regular naval position in early 1957 and Cmdr. Ed Holley became the eighth leader since the team's conception.

Even before 1957 the world of subsonic and transonic aircraft had been giving way to the newer, more glamourous aircraft of the supersonic class. After two and one-half years of proud service with the team, the F9F-8 Cougars were to be replaced by a member of the supersonic stable. The team tested several newer aircraft, deciding on the Grumman F11A Tiger.

An April 5 show at NAS El Centro marked the Blue Angels' last performance in the swept-winged Cougars. Each pilot walked away from the last F9F-8 demonstration with a mixture of feelings - a degree of sadness in parting with a "bird" who had shared their lives and kept them safe - and yet, a restless anticipation in converting the unique characteristics of a newer "cat" into the composite perfection of flight.

Blue Angel #1 sits on the ramp at NAS Los Alamitos, California. Fans in the area were treated to two shows during the 1955 season as the team performed in March before 100,000 and again in July before 70,000. Note that only the Panther and Cougar series of Blue Angel aircraft carried the U.S. Navy lettering on the forward area of the fuselages and only the Cougar ever carried the team name on the rear of the aircraft.

A solo Cougar barrels beneath the four-ship echelon on the fast-slow pass. In this maneuver the echelon had slowed to 150 mph while #5 roared across at 450 mph.

Crew chiefs stand ready during recovery as the Blues return to NAS Corpus Christi following a morning practice.

Skimming low over the blue-green water of the Gulf of Mexico, the diamond displays the five-foot wing over wing separation used during demonstrations.

Posing above their namesake in early 1955 are Lt. Nello Pierozzi, Cmdr. Zeke Cormier, Lt. Ken Wallace, and Lt. Bill Gureck.

The fleur-de-lis, a maneuver originating with the 1953 team and destined to become a trademark of the Blue Angels.

Photos shot over the Gulf always produced excellent PR results, but flying a show over the water was always most difficult for the pilots due to a lack of visual references for timing purposes.

Three Cougars frame their "bosses" and "keepers." These "adopted Texans" would migrate to a new home a few months later.

Ralph Donnell, chief test pilot for Grumman, and Lt. Pierozzi look over some photos and reports during a team visit to Bethpage, N.Y.

Climbing aboard for a 30-minute endurance test, or as the Blues called it, a normal practice session.

Once she made the team, the Cougar flew 105 demonstrations before turning her role over to another "cat."

In a world of their own ... the Blue Angels appear suspended between the thick white clouds below them and the brilliant blue of the sky around them.

Date	# of Days	Locality	Attendance	Occasion	6 1956
3-10	1	Reno, Nevada	4000	Nevada Day	
3-25	1	NAS New Orleans	25000	Open House	
4-6	1	NAAS Chase Field	10000	Open House	
4-7	1	NAS Corpus Christi	40000	Navy Relief Carnival	
4-12	1	NAS Birmingham	30000	Open House	
4-15	1	NAAS Barin Field	12000	Open House	
4-27	1	Cleveland, Ohio	50,000	Dedication of Airport	
4-28	1	Cleveland, Ohio	30,000	Dedication of Airport	
5-5	1	Pensacola, Fla.	5000	Fiesta of Five Flags	
5-12	1	Los Alamitos, Cal.	90000	Open House	
5-13	1	Wide Wide World	TV Audience	Nation Wide U.S.S. Essex	
5-22	1	Washington, D.C.	65000	Armed Forces Day	
5-23	1	Hunter AFB	40,000	Open House	
5-26	1	Akron, Ohio	15000		
6-2&3	2	Santa Ana, Cal.	19000	State Model Meet	
6-10	1	Peconic River	50000		
6-15	1	Quonset Point	5000		
6-16-17	2	NAS Memphis	80,000		
6-26	1	NAS Atlantic City	4000	Goveners Conference	
7-4	1	South Weymouth	50000		
7-8	1	NAS Glenview	150,000		
7-14	1	Quonset Point	30000		
7-21	1	NAS Corpus Christi	5000		
7-28-29	2	NAS Dallas, Texas	200,000		
8-5	1	NAS Seattle, Wash.	650,000	Sea Fair	
8-11	1	NAS Corpus Christi	7000		
8-18	1	NAS Denver	110000		
9-(1-2-3)	3	Oklahoma City	176,000	National Ac-ft Show	
9-7&8	2	Toronto, Canada	476,000	Int. Nat. Ac-ft Show	

A copy of a page from the Blues log book. Note the variety of events which drew requests for a Blue Angel appearance, including a TV show and the first demonstration in Canada.

Pulled into a tight diamond, each pilot must make constant minor adjustments with his flight controls to compensate for both the presence of the other aircraft and the uneven air currents generated from the hot desert floor below.

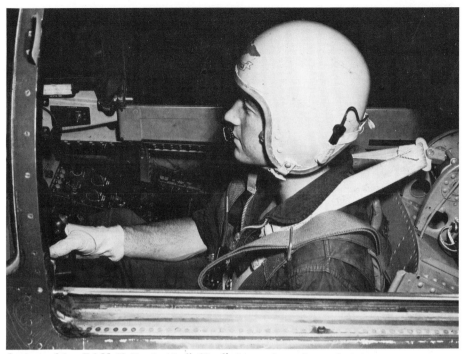

A view of Lt. Ed McKeller in his "office" shows that a jet cockpit is a tight fit, with no allowances for claustrophobia once the canopy is closed.

The work's all done for another day . . . now comes the fun of shaking hands, answering questions, and signing autographs.

Pilots of the prop days often claimed that left wing was the hardest position to fly but with jets the hardest "tag" went to the "tail-end Charlie" better known as slot.

Best seat in the house for a show was the control tower . . . a great photography platform, 360° view and radio contact with the team.

El Centro, California, served as the winter training home for the team during January and February of 1954-1957.

Harry Burns, photographer for Grumman, records the clear details of the Cougar in this underneath shot. Only the horizontal stabilizers, cambered wing edges, intake rims and ARA-25 radio domes of the other aircraft, are visable above the slot plane. Note the oil line running along the underside of the jet.

Folded wings and a friendly wave during 1956-57 winter training from Cmdr. Cormier (in Gureck's aircraft), Lt. Chuck Holloway, Lt. Bill Gureck and Cmdr. Ed Holley. The narrator's TV-2 sits farther down the line.

The white sands of the north Florida coast stand out beneath the blue and gold jets as the team passes through the top of a loop at 7,000 feet.

Diving down the backside of a change-over loop.

A view that would make the average earthling dizzy is a part of the everyday upside down world of the Blue Angel pilot as he plays follow the leader through a barrel roll.

Ernest Borgnine listens with interest to Cmdr. Ed Holley's "hangar flying." Borgnine has been a friend of the Blues since 1955 and the filming of "Navy Log."

Cmdr. Cormier leads the Blues in a test flight of the North American FJ-4 Fury over Columbus, Ohio. This aircraft was considered as a 1957 replacement for the F9F-8 but lost out to the F11A Tiger.

LAST OF THE CATS
The F11A

The Blues and the F11A Tiger first became a pair in mid-1957. The combination would become inseperable for more than 10 years, the longest duty put in by any single type aircraft in the team's history.

This "cat" came with a reputation. Not only would she be the first Blues' jet capable of sustained Mach-plus flight but she was an aerodynamic innovator in being the first aircraft to adopt the "area rule" principle more often referred to as the "coke bottle" fuselage. During the Tiger era the team would trade their original short-nosed F11As for a newer, long-nosed version, and Grumman and her own Blue Angel maintenance personnel would identify her with three paint schemes.

The short-nosed F11A was flown by the team from May 1957 until the end of the 1958 season with the long-nosed version serving from 1959 through the 1968 season.

Both versions of the Tiger were powered by a Wright J65 engine which provided 10,500 lbs of thrust including afterburner power. They could reach a speed of 750 mph in level flight and operate to an altitude of 41,000 feet. Weighing in at 13,307 lbs the short-nosed version spread her weight over a span of 31' 8", a length of 45' 5", and a height of 13' 3" while her long-nosed younger sister divided it over a span of 31' 8", a length of 46' 11", and a height of 13' 3".

With the advent of the Tiger, a completely new solo demonstration evolved as the team went to a dual solo routine. This addition of a second solo also allowed the Blue Angels to develop a variety of six-ship delta maneuvers.

In 1959 the team, now led by Cmdr. Zeb Knott, added Bermuda to its foreign show sites as they performed there before 25,000 spectators, including the Duke of Edinburgh.

Under the leadership of Cmdr. Ken Wallace during the 1962-63 seasons, the team began the intricate and impressive diamond and delta landings, and in the air, added the farvel to the diamond, and the half-Cuban eight to the solo routines. Especially proud moments during these years came at a September 1962 show before President John Kennedy and at NAS Lemoore, California, in 1963 when the Blue Angels celebrated their 1,000th demonstration.

The team had a chance to show off their supersonic Tigers before a record, single-day show crowd of 1,500,000 on July 26, 1964, in Mexico City, Mexico. Led by Cmdr. Bob Aumack, who would continue as the "boss" through the 1966 season, the Blues continued their overseas deployments with a spring Caribbean trip, a summer 25-day European tour, and a fall deployment to the Bahamas, all during the 1965 season.

The Caribbean trip consisted of five shows flown at Andros Island, Nassau, Puerto Rico, and Jamaica before 65,000 fans. More than 575,000 people viewed the sleek F11As roaring through their paces as the team displayed its talent at numerous show sites in France, England, Finland, Denmark, Holland and Iceland. Following the Blue Angels' return to the United States, a special letter of commendation was read into the Congressional Record on the Senate floor in recognition of the team's performance at the Paris Air Show while on the European trip.

The last few show days of the 1965 season saw the team fly two shows in the Bahamas for an audience of 25,000.

Cmdr. Bill Wheat would be the last commander to lead the Blues in the F11A. Shortly after he assumed command in early 1967, the team departed for a second European tour. Starting the tour in mid-May with three shows in Italy, the team thrilled spectators with three additional performances in Tunisia, Turkey and France. The final Paris show was flown on June 4th before a crowd of 500,000.

In August of the same year they demonstrated their aerial ballet for three shows at Abbotsford, British Columbia, Canada.

Two short deployments in 1968 took the team to Nova Scotia, Canada and Puerto Rico. The last performance of the 1968 season was flown at NAS El Centro, California. To most it would have appeared to be no different from the other 71 shows that year. But for the pilots and enlisted personnel it again marked a time for parting with an old friend.

Time had caught up with the F11A, as with all her predecessors. Just as she had waited in the wings to replace the F9F-8, another newer, more sophisticated craft waited to take her place. But this parting was different from the others because for the first time in Blue Angel history the next plane to wear the blue and gold would not be a "cat."

Grumman had been as much a part of the Blue Angels as the team had been a part of Grumman. Now, after 22 years, each was going its own way. Many were saddened at the parting but their nostalgia would always remain. Each "cat" had performed its duty with as much pride and excellence as the men who flew them and the Blue Angels had 22 years of history to represent that pride.

At Grumman to take a close-up look at the Tiger before taking the new "cat" home.

The F11As show off their distinctive Angel colors. Tail numbers must still be added; note the Blue Angels name in script on the intake.

Lights — Action — Camera . . . .

1957: Making a Grumman public relations film.

Playing hide and seek with right wing. The perfect alignment allows only the pitot tube of #2 to indicate his presence. During 1958 the team name appeared in block letters along the intake.

"Me and my shadow . . . ."

Looking more like a softball team about to take the field, the support personnel get instructions on a new piece of equipment during winter training at Key West.

The short-nosed Tigers can be recognized from below by the solid arrow-like paint design under the nose.

Pulling into a reverse echelon roll.

November 1958: Arrival of the first long-nosed F11A.

Ray Hiller, Dave Scheuer, Lt. Jack Dewenter, and Lt. John Damian inspect the exhaust of a dormant volcano.

Standing four Tigers on their tails.

Cmdr. Zeb Knott gets everyone in the act.

Grumman rep Dave Scheuer checks out a problem on the left panel of the #1 aircraft.

1960: Actors stand with some of the planes used during the filming of the TV series "Blue Angels." The series advisor was Cmdr. Zeke Cormier and some 39 episodes were filmed.

One mile from crowd center ... lined up for a left echelon roll ... and everybody is tucked in tight.

Over the nation's capital.

Wheels down . . . and locked!

Before a morning workout #1 gets the usual pampered attention of a star. A ground crew of 45-55 people were required during the F11A years.

When the world is right side up for the lead solo (#5) it's upside down for everyone else. Note that the long-nosed Tigers carried the team name in script on the nose with the Blue Angels decal on the intake.

Brakes off . . . diamond rolling . . . NOW!

Past the Golden Gate and San Francisco.

Heading home from an over-the-Gulf practice.

Approaching for a left echelon roll. The book says the maneuver cannot be done . . . the Blues have performed it since their Bearcat days.

Like speeding bullets, the solos put her on the deck and roar by at 600 mph.

"Up, up the long delirious, burning blue . . . ."

Stern critics from the Blue Angels maintenance team enjoy a 1961 performance by their aerial brothers, the USAF Thunderbirds. During this period the Thunderbirds were flying the North American F100-C Super Sabre.

The diamond passes Mt. Rainier as they head eastward from a demonstration at Seattle.

An A-6 Intruder serves as a high-flying gas station for #1 as #3 holds a distant right wing position.

1961 -- Fifteen years beyond the Bearcat.

A saguaro cactus "snaps a salute" as the diamond lays a smoke trail across the Arizona desert. From 1963 through 1966 the Blue Angels spent their winter training months in the Grand Canyon state.

Lt. Cmdr. Ken Wallace finds the Easter bunny has visited prior to a Sunday holiday air show.

August 1962: Lt. Cmdr. Wallace presents a Blue Angel model to President John Kennedy following the team's 939th demonstration.

Each year the team participates in the Pensacola Five Flags Fiesta. Over the years a warm relationship has developed between the team and the townfolk.

In this farvel shot, the elongated polished metal sections seen below U.S. Navy are areas where oil mist gathers along the fuselage. The team found it easier from a maintenance standpoint to keep the area unpainted.

The F11As were the first Blue Angel aircraft to be flown in delta formation. Over the years the individual delta maneuvers have varied but the six-ship formation remains as much a crowd pleaser today as during the 1960s.

A 1962 trip to Grumman puts Lt. Dan MacIntyre into an earth-bound simulator.

NAS Lemoore, California, throws the Blue Angels a July 4th, 1963, celebration for their 1,000th show - though it would not be flown until their next demonstration two days later at Pocatello, Idaho.

The two solo Tigers drop into wing positions on the slot as the team shifts into a delta variation - the double V.

Aerial map briefings are the first step at any show site. They provide the pilots with details of terrain, show check-point markers and any local obstacles.

At NAS Memphis, the sleek "cats" taxi toward the active runway and into take-off position.

Recovery taxi following a 1965 performance in France. Thousands of Frenchmen wait behind boundary ropes to say hello and request autographs.

During the 1965 trip to Europe the Tigers always displayed the host country's flag from the pitot tube while the narrator's Cougar carried the American flag. Standing with pride beside an F11A at Vichey, France, are Cmdr. Bob Aumack, Lt. Bob McDonough, Lt. Red Hubbard, Lt. Frank Mezzadri, Lt. Cmdr. Dick Oliver and Capt. Fred Craig.

Drinking a toast with host Capt. Phillipe DeGaulle, son of Gen. Charles DeGaulle.

London . . . and the tower "Big Ben" . . . .

Stacked in an in-trail formation. When brought down to the deck, this formation served as the entrance to the three-in-one maneuver.

The roar of Tigers . . . .

Meeting people is as much a part of the Blues' demonstrations as putting 13,300 lb jet planes through their paces.

With canopy back, Capt. Craig taxies in following a 1966 show at the Calverton Air Show in New York.

At any show site the team's arrival draws representatives from the various media with note pads, tape recorders and TV cameras ready.

Gov. Ronald Reagan receives a colorful lithograph from Cmdr. Bill Wheat and the 1967 team following a show at Orange County Airport, California.

1957 - 1968: The "cat" with 11½ lives.

No heavenly angel could ever receive more dedicated attention than these earth-assigned, mechanical ones.

AWESOME ANGEL

The F-4J

In December 1968 the officers and enlisted personnel of the Blue Angels began their own saga of the "Beauty and the Beast." From the moment of the F-4J's arrival, the symmetry of her blue and gold outline defined an image of airborne beauty to every pilot's heart. But buried within that beauty was the power of a beast never flown before or since by the Blue Angels.

This new "beast" was the first McDonnell Douglas aircraft to be used by the team - she carried the name Phantom II. With her two GE J-79 engines, a total of 34,000 lbs of thrust including afterburner, could propel the 44,000 lb fighter-bomber at speeds of more than 1,600 mph to altitudes of 100,000 feet. Never mistaken along a flight line for any other plane in the Navy inventory, the Phantom II distinctively displayed her beauty in a frame with a span of 38' 5", a length of 58' 3", and a height of 16' 6".

Modifications on the F-4Js to aerial demonstration requirements included ballast weight substituted for the fire control system, VHF radio additions, the positioning of afterburner selection at 89% of engine speed instead of the usual 94%, a modification for additional inverted flight and the modification of the forward AAM "Sparrows" to carry oil and the rear AAMs to carry dye.

With the Phantom II came new maneuvers for the 1969 show season. The diamond added a trail loop and box loop formation while the solos began performing opposing four-point rolls and inverted half-Cuban eights. More than four million fans in the United States and Canada had viewed the team and their new jets by the end of their first F-4J season.

Cmdr. Harley Hall replaced Cmdr. Wheat in 1970 and the new maneuvers continued, including the line-abreast loop, tuck under break, inverted fleur-de-lis, opposing solo dirty rolls on take off and the solo dirty loop. In addition to the usual demonstrations in the continental United States and Canada the 1970 season included short trips to Puerto Rico, Panama, Ecuador and Hawaii.

The team celebrated their 25th anniversary the following year with 94 air shows including a return visit to the Pacific. From October 21 to November 25, their first Far East tour took them to Korea, Japan, Taiwan, the Philippines and Guam for a total of 13 shows before almost two million spectators.

Cmdr. Don Bently lead the Blues through the 1972 season and the early months of 1973 before a non-fatal accident caused him to relinquish the #1 position to Lt. Cmdr. Skip Umstead in April.

Under Lt. Cmdr. Umstead the team again traveled to Europe. Between May 24 and June 17 they flew a total of 13 shows in England, France, Spain, Turkey, Iran and Italy. One short trip in early July took them to Nassau, Bahamas. A tragic accident during arrival maneuvers at Lakehurst, New Jersey, on July 26 resulted in the deaths of Lt. Cmdr. Umstead, Capt. Mike Murphy, and crew chief ADJ 1 Ronald Thomas. The team immediately cancelled the remaining 22 shows of the season.

The Phantom II had been a part of the team's history for five years. Probably no other aircraft had been or would ever be as impressive for public demonstrations but the cost of maintaining and fueling the F-4J had become prohibitive. During the latter months of the shortened 1973 season the decision was made to transition from the F-4J to a smaller, more economical aircraft for the 1974 demonstrations.

McDonnell Douglas would provide another in the Phantom's place but as the blue and gold colors were removed from her many surfaces to be replaced with a more operational Navy paint scheme, part of the aerial impact at air shows went with it. The Blues' colors could be put on another fine, capable successor, but the "beast" had made its impression to pilot and public alike and her "beauty" in vari-colored smoke trails would evoke memories in many a spectator in the years ahead.

Capt. Vince Donile signs a lithograph for a McDonnell Douglas employee as the team visits the plant for a look at their new F-4Js.

The "beast" required a support crew of 97 of which about 35 traveled to any single show site.

Cleaning off the windscreen following a morning outing over El Centro. Note the Phantom still lacks a tail number. The refuel boom stretches above the right intake.

"Now the book says. . . ."

As the farvel passes overhead one gets a good look at the four AAMs. The forward blue pair carrying oil for white smoke are harder to detect than the rear gold pair carrying the red and blue dye.

The visor of slot pilot Lt. Christensen reflects the diamond aircraft ahead of him while on each side of his canopy can be seen the wingtips of #5 and #6 as the team flies in a delta formation.

Anyone who took a back seat PR ride with the narrator during the Phantom years wound up with an unforgettable experience.

The Phantom II's great, great grandfather shows its stuff in its version of a high speed pass.

Lt. Ernie Christensen, slot, makes a little lady's day.

"Four's down . . . . "

March 1970: The eyes of Puerto Rico are on the Blues while right wing, left wing and slot all have their eyes glued on #1.

Lead solo Lt. Steve Shoemaker lifts off as the opposing solo does the same from the opposite end of the runway. The result is a spectacular opposing dirty roll on takeoff.

Approaching the break point for the fleur-de-lis.

The Phantom IIs were the only aircraft flown by both the Blue Angels and USAF Thunderbirds. Each team used the planes from 1969-1973 with the Thunderbirds flying the F-4E while the Blues used the F-4J.

Whether on a tour of Europe or at air shows in North America, a British Vulcan demonstration often preceded one by the Blues.

"Can I fly in the rear seat of your Phantom?"

Over the top at 8,000 feet and down the backside of a delta loop.

#6 going to work before a show crowd in late 1970.

During winter training #6 heads for the practice area to break in her new pilot, Lt. Skip Umstead.

By mid-February #6 joins ranks with her sisters to practice a delta maneuver.

Cmdr. Hall exits #1. One of the Blue Angels' most popular leaders, Hall would leave the Blue Angels at the end of the 1971 season returning to Vietnam for a third combat tour where he would become the last Navy pilot to be shot down and killed on the last day of the war.

One of the toughest maneuvers to fly -- the line-abreast loop.

Climbing through a change-over roll. At the top of the roll the aircraft will shift from the right echelon formation into a diamond.

The team takes several minutes following a landing to meet for a short mini-debrief before walking toward the eager fans waiting for autographs.

The F-4J was a photographer's delight, but earplugs were a must.

A rarer five-ship formation. This was a variation of the delta formation when illness or a serious maintenance problem prevented the team from having its usual six aircraft available.

From canopy to wingtip -- a 36 inch separation.

Cmdr. Harley Hall rolls into the tuck under break with Capt. Kevin O'Mara about to follow.

By the Phantom era a Blue Angel demonstration lasted 45 minutes, twice the length of the pre-Korea days.

COLOR GALLERY

F8F-1 Bearcat

F9F-5 Panthers

F9F-8 Cougar

F11A Tiger

F-4 Phantom II

A-4F Skyhawk

C-130F Hercules, better known as Fat Albert

A-4F Skyhawk, over the USS Lexington at NAS Pensacola

As awesome from the back as from the front.

Tail-end Charlie slides into position with an ever-so-gentle nudge of the control stick.

Lt. Umstead and Lt. Bill Switzer streak past one another at speeds of more than 500 mph as they perform the knife edge pass.

On their 1971 trip to the Far East the Blue Angels get a first-class tourist's view of Mt. Fuji in Japan.

Returning from the Far East the team flies the last show of their 1971 season at Nellis AFB, Nevada. The gear on #4 is almost fully retracted as he slides into the slot on take off.

Lt. Cmdr. Don Bently ejecting from his disabled F-4J at Kingston, North Carolina in July 1972.

Holding formation the diamond clears the area as the solos begin another pass before the crowd line.

One second flat on the deck, the next second straight up on twin tails of flame.

Getting ready for their walk-down, the attention of the Blues is caught by another performer at the show site.

Riding a plume of smoke the team holds a difficult in-trail position.

The roar of four Phantoms could raise the hair on the back of anyone's neck.

Narrator Lt. Gary Smith provides the spectators with a constant, colorful explanation of the team's maneuvers and mission. The tape recorder allows for a later review of his timing with the sequence of events.

Bottoming out of a line-abreast loop. In this maneuver the lead Phantom is second from the left with #2 on his right and #3 and #4 to his left.

A thing of beauty in the hands of the Blue Angels - a diamond landing.

A NOBLE BREED OF HAWK
The A—4F

By the beginning of the 1974 season the Blue Angels not only had a different look, but also a new designation. In late 1973 the U.S. Navy reorganized the unit from a flight demonstration team into a flight demonstration squadron. During the transition Capt. Ken Wallace returned for his third tour to serve as program manager, while Cmdr. Tony Less took over the reins as flight leader and began molding the newest Angel aircraft to the team's exacting requirements.

The newly-formed, tradition-old squadron continued work as always with dedicated practice both on the ground and in the air. Their new chariots were half the cost of the previous F-4Js, required 65% - 75% less fuel and required less maintenance hours and a smaller maintenance crew.

Some called the new addition "Scooter," others knew the plane by the affectionate nickname of "Mighty Midget," but she was officially the McDonnell Douglas A-4F Skyhawk II. Looking almost dainty along a flight line where the shadows of her larger F-4J cousins were remembered, she stood slightly nose-high on her long forward gear and awaited her place as a part of Blue Angel history.

Though smaller than her predecessor, the A-4F was well suited to the team's needs and took to the demonstration role as if an old hand. A powerful Pratt and Whitney J52-P-408 engine creating a thrust of 11,200 lbs pushed her through her paces at speeds up to 650 mph and an altitude of 47,900 feet. One-fourth the weight of the Phantom at 11,000 lbs, the Skyhawk II distributed her weight over a span of 27' 6", a length of 40' 3", and a height of 15 feet.

Modifications were required in her inverted fuel, pilot restraint and elevator fuel systems, as well as a strengthening of the outboard aileron hinge fittings. Other changes included the addition of the VHF radio, a drogue chute, a built-in fold-ladder, and a smoke system.

On May 18 the Blue Angels made their first public appearance in their new steeds at Omaha, Nebraska. A total of 52 demonstrations were recorded during the 1974 season. With the 1975 season the team returned to its usual March-November schedule and performed 69 shows.

The nation's bicentennial year saw Cmdr. Casey Jones replace Cmdr. Tony Less. Helping America to celebrate her birthday, the Blue Angels flew 80 demonstrations including two in Puerto Rico, three at Abbotsford, British Columbia, Canada, and one in California celebrating the team's 30th anniversary reunion.

Part of a busy 1977 schedule included two spring shows in Puerto Rico and two summer shows at Hamilton, Ontario, Canada. On October 8, the Blue Angels flew their 2,000th demonstration at NAS Atlanta, Georgia.

Cmdr. Bill Newman joined the team in 1978 as the Blues' 17th commander/leader. The team's schedule of 75 shows again took them to Abbotsford, B.C., Canada.

Now in their 33rd season, the team is again on the road fulfilling a schedule of more than 70 demonstrations. Their first show in Yuma, Arizona, was their 2089th. They continue to add to the more than 130 million spectators who have seen them since that first show long ago over Jacksonville, Florida.

Some shows, as always, will be rained out, others the weather will reduce from the normal high show to a flat or low show. But wherever the Blue Angels appear they will continue to impress their audiences. Among new fans at each site are youngsters who stand beside fathers or grandfathers as the elders relate when they first saw the Blues in their F8F-1 Bearcats or F9F-8 Cougars.

Many youngsters dream of being a Blue Angel. Along those flight lines stand many of the Blue Angels of the years to come. Some are not youngsters but mature, expert pilots of the present who will be selected this year or in the next few years to join the team. These new members -- officers or enlisted -- will arrive with the same enthusiasm as their predecessors. They will spend two months at winter training and follow those months with nine grueling, but rewarding, months on the road. They will meet new fans and old fans, future Blues and former Blues who built a tradition of which they have become a part.

Each Blue Angel carries a lot of pride. He should. That pride is built in knowing that, not only is he doing his job as expertly as it can be performed, but for 33 years those who carried the same name and wore the same patch have provided the pride which makes any Blue Angel a respected representative of the U.S. Navy and a proud example of American aviation history.

The diamond breaks into a climb and the solos begin their horizontal rolls in a six-ship version of the fleur-de-lis. Until 1977 the maneuver was performed with five aircraft.

Accelerating to 500 mph the solos streak past one another as the diamond eases along with flaps, gear and tail hooks extended during a slow/fast pass.

Upside down at 7,500 feet a tilt of the head backwards gives a better view of the ground above you.

A quick retraction of the gear on take off leaves #6 suspended above a plume of smoke. Within seconds the Skyhawk will have enough altitude for her pilot to put her into a breath-taking clean roll.

The only thing more impressive than the diamond landing is the delta landing.

All opposing solo passes draw gasps from spectators as the planes
appear to collide. In actuality, the A-4Fs are separated both
horizontally and vertically at a safe distance from one another.

With each pilot pulling 4Gs, the Skyhawks complete one of their most spectacular maneuvers, the delta loop.

May 1974: During his vice presidency, Gerald Ford visits with the Blue Angels.

Traveling at 500 mph the two solos practice an approach into the solo spacer maneuver.

Cmdr. Tony Less begins a cockpit check as his crew chief assists. Before the helmet goes on, Less must put on a skull cap to protect him from irritation.

Still flying a maneuver the manual says can't be done . . . a left echelon roll.

Many show sites during a season do not have runways wide enough for a delta landing. For the ones that do, the thousands of spectators are treated to an unforgettable display of precision flying.

In 1977 the line-abreast maneuver became a five-ship formation, making it even tougher to fly and more impressive to watch.

1976: Cmdr. Casey Jones shares the cockpit of a Tudor jet with the Snowbirds commander/leader Maj. Denis Gauthier.

The neighboring team to the north . . . Canada's Snowbirds.

Lt. Mike Curtin rotates #6 and begins his role in a 45-minute aerial ballet. Several months later a fatal accident during arrival maneuvers at NAS Miramar, California, would end the career of one of the Navy's finest aviators.

Popping the silk insures a shorter roll on runways of less length than the team's normal landing parameters.

At most show sites the Blues share the stage with a variety of demonstration aircraft. Here a Marine Harrier jet maintains a hovering position, only one of many unusual flight attitudes of which the plane is capable.

The solos break into a 360-degree turn as the diamond continues upward and beyond the crowd's view in a beautiful maneuver called the delta head-on opener.

Caught midway between three opposing horizontal rolls.

Mirror of the present ... echoes of the past.

From a vertical double "V" formation the Skyhawks break toward six points of the compass.

Following a half-Cuban 8 reversal each jet streaks back across the center point as the six Skyhawks converge at a closing speed of more than 1,000 mph. Note the truck below the crossing jets. It serves as the pilots' visual reference for the center point.

A recognizable maneuver, the farvel. Beginning with the 1979 season the slot Skyhawk also maintained an inverted position and the maneuver was renamed the double farvel.

Framed against the snowy backdrop of the Sierras, six Hawks invade territory usually reserved for eagles.

Solo pilot Lt. Jerry Tucker enters his "office" to begin a very concentrated work day. Tucker is presently serving a second tour as the lead solo. This photo is from the 1974 season.

Photographed from the TA-4J the delta begins a landing approach with gear down and speed brakes extended.

Sections of the instrument panel and windshield reflect in the visor of a helmet worn by only a select few and desired by thousands of aviators.

Public relations activities go beyond flying planes and signing autographs. A good-natured challenge at a western show site puts two of the Blues' enlisted personnel behind the plate.

When rain threatens, the canopies are protected by covers quickly put into place by the crew chiefs.

A slight nudge of the controls by slot and right wing, and the delta will be in perfect alignment.

The bright Puerto Rican sun reflects off the highly polished leading edges as the team taxies in following a 1974 show at NAS Roosevelt Roads.

Back-to-back with overlapped wings, the solos perform the popular fortus maneuver at better than 200 mph.

Blues narrator Lt. Bruce Davey and events coordinator Lt. Ray Sandelli at work during a 1977 air show.

The maintenance officer, Lt. Jack Johnson, maintains constant verbal contact with the pilots during every demonstration.

With the tools of his trade in hand, team photographer PH1 John Porter moves across the field toward show center.

Lead's off ... the wingmen begin rotation ... and Lt. Cmdr. Bruce Davey tucks the nose of #4 downward in preparation for a rapid lift off and acceleration into the slot position.

Keep on truckin'!

Cmdr. Casey Jones leads his troops through one of the seven wonders of the world . . . the Grand Canyon.

A happy young fan hands a 1979 yearbook to events coordinator Lt. Kent Horne for signing after an April show at Davis-Monthan AFB, Arizona.

"Fat Albert" provides shade as maintenance officer Lt. Ben Woods and maintenance chief ADCS Hector Alverez give last-minute instructions before a demonstration launch.

The jets prepare to launch for home as rain washes out a Sunday show. Two of the road crew sprint across the wet runway to return a starter unit to the dry innards of "Fat Albert."

Solo pilot Lt. Jim Ross and crew chief AE1 Joe Berry are interviewed by a talk show hostess for a Corpus Christi television station.

McDonnell Douglas tech rep Dale Specht inspects a bird hit on the left intake of the lead solo aircraft. The incident occurred during a Friday practice show over the St. Petersburg, Florida, airport.

A videotape is made of every performance -- practice or public -- and is closely scrutinized in a thorough debrief following each show.

May 12, 1979: President Jimmy Carter, a former Navy officer who once experienced a PR back seat ride while governor of Georgia, congratulates the Blue Angels on their 33rd year as ambassadors of good will.

Internal problems in the left wing of the #6 Skyhawk calls for a multi-man work force from the Blues' road crew.

As repairs progress on the upper wing surface, production chief AMSC Larry Netherton lends a hand from below.

Right wing Capt. Fred Stankovich signs an autograph before joining his fellow pilots near the A-4Fs.

Crew chief of the #7 jet AMH1 Jim Talbot answers questions from an interested spectator who looks over the array of dials and switches in the modern day aircraft.

Many times the Blues have provided maintenance assistance to the USAF Thunderbirds. The favor is returned during a Blues visit to the Thunderbirds' home base, Nellis AFB, Nevada, in 1977.

The Blue Angels follow the path of "Ole Man River" which takes them past such St. Louis landmarks as Busch Stadium and the Gateway Arch.

"Those magnificent men in their flying machines, they go uppety-up-up . . .

. . . they go down-dity-down-down."

BEST ANGEL IN A SUPPORTING ROLE

At any present day air show the spectators' attention is often drawn to two aircraft sitting separate from the six A-4Fs. Both carry the Blue Angel name and colors though one is a multiengined C-130F Hercules and the other is a TA-4J Skyhawk II. Just as important to the team's mission as the six A-4F demonstration jets, these are the Blue Angel support aircraft. Each represents a lengthy line of notable ancestors.

The first of these was a North American SNJ which the team used from the second Hellcat show until September 1949. The plane, painted yellow and red, was used as a Japanese "Zero" for a simulated dogfight at each show site. By 1948 she was affectionately known as "Beetle Bomb." Between shows the small primary trainer was used by the narrator for transportation.

With the transition to the F9F-2, a Bearcat was selected to continue the combat role of the SNJ. Also given the name "Beetle Bomb," she performed in her support role until the team was disbanded for Korea.

When the Blue Angels were reformed following their combat tour, two new jet support aircraft were added to the team. During the 1952 season Chance Vought F7U-1 Cutlass jets were used as dual solos while a Lockheed TV-2 Shooting Star joined the team as the narrator's steed. The F7U-1s proved to be an excessive maintenance problem and were quickly replaced by two additional F9F-5 Panthers. In contrast, the TV-2 served faithfully through the Panther and Cougar years until its replacement in mid-1957 with an F9F-8T Cougar.

The new Cougar was a twin-seated trainer version of the F9F-8 demonstration jet and was used by the team throughout the F11A Tiger era. During that time her designation was altered from an F9F-8T to a TF-9J and a #7 replaced the #0 on her tail.

In 1969 the Blue Angels transitioned to the F-4J Phantom II and for the first time in the team's history the narrator's aircraft became the same as that used by the demonstration pilots. The same policy continued with the move to the A-4F in 1974, except that the narrator flies a twin-seater TA-4J version of the Skyhawk II.

While the team's tradition of various demonstration and narrator's aircraft was evolving, so was a colorful history of their transport aircraft.

During the Blues' pre-Korea years no specific transports were assigned to the team. The maintenance crews traveling to the various show sites were ferried on any R5C Skytrain or R4D Commando available at the time from their home base. Even after their reactivation in 1951 the team continued to use a non-specific variety of R4D, R5C and R5D aircraft.

Noting the team's need for a permanent multiengined support aircraft, the Navy assigned a Douglas R5D Skymaster to the team in late 1961. She was to fly exclusively as a Blue Angel carrying the team's colors as well as their patch. The Skymaster quickly developed a number of nicknames, such as the "Lead Sled." Putting in many faithful years and hundreds of thousands of air miles, she served on the team until 1968. She was replaced by a larger, faster Lockheed C-121J Super Constellation.

The "Connie" was also on permanent assignment and wore her distinctive colors until her replacement in 1970 by the first of three Lockheed C-130F Hercules. Quickly dubbed "Fat Albert," the first C-130F was painted white except for certain areas painted black, with the standard Blue Angel logo on the tail. In April 1973 a second C-130F replaced the first one and served with the team until April 1974. At that time the third and present C-130F was assigned to the squadron. Still called "Fat Albert," he was painted in the popular blue, gold and white colors. The transition from the C-121J to the C-130F resulted in a major change in the duty role of the team's maintenance officer. Since 1958 he not only had responsibility for the operational status of all aircraft and maintenance personnel assigned to the team but he had also flown the transport aircraft. The change to "Fat Albert" meant not only the arrival of a new plane, but also the arrival of a Marine flight crew assigned as an integral part of the Blues' team. The C-130F crew consists of three pilots, two flight engineers, a navigator, a flight mechanic and a radio operator/loadmaster.

These support aircraft of the past and present may never have been or will be the "stars" at any Blue Angel air show. But their history is just as varied, just as proud, and just as important as their sister demonstration aircraft. Somehow, when you watch a newsman's face crack into a wide grin as he climbs down from a back seat PR ride or hear a little girl's giggle as she stares up at "Fat Albert's" bubble nose, you find yourself thinking, "maybe the supporting role is actually a starring one after all."

The North American SNJ painted for her role as a "Zero." She made her appearance at the second Blue Angel show at NAS Corpus Christi in 1946 and was replaced by an F8F-1 in 1949. During a show, smoke was released as the F6Fs or F8Fs simulated an attack and a crewman riding in the rear seat threw out a dummy to give the appearance of the pilot bailing out. Only one pilot was ever specifically assigned to fly the SNJ. After Lt. (jg) Stouse left the team the plane was flown by any new officer until an opening occurred in the diamond or solo positions.

"Beetle Bomb," the SNJ's replacement. More than 200 mph faster than the SNJ, she served in her support role until the team's reassignment to combat in 1950.

In 1952 the team tried using two F7U-1 Cutlass twin-engined jets as solos. Flown at only two air shows, Glenview, Illinois, and Detroit, Michigan, the aircraft proved to be an excessive maintenance problem and were dropped from the team.

Following Korea, the team's narrator flew the Lockheed TV-2 Shooting Star until the Blues received the F11As in mid-1957.

A Cougar PR ride could put a smile on the face and butterflies in the stomach.

The #0 Cougar, an F9F-8T, was the team's first while the later "Dash-Eight" carried the #7 and was designated a TF-9J.

Lining up for a long drink. The arrow design under the nose dates the Cougar from the long-nosed F11A period. During those years the arrows were two colors, while during the short-nosed Tiger period the arrow was a solid yellow.

Cub Scouts in Yuma, Arizona, get a feel of what it's like to snuggle into the rear seat of #7.

113

Between 1946 and 1961, the team had no transport plane assigned to it. The road crews traveled in whatever R5C, R4D, or R5D aircraft was available at their home base. Here they are seen loading a Curtiss R5C Commando.

1958: One of the Douglas R5D Skymasters traveling with the Blues. Note the team decal under the cockpit window.

Another "borrowed" R5D. Note the addition of the team name near the decal.

In her team colors first applied in 1961, the R5D Skymaster stands at tie-down between hauling jobs.

The "Lead Sled" on the road.

In Puerto Rico for three shows in March 1970 the C-121J was about six weeks away from being replaced by the team's first C-130F.

In her first year with the team, the "Connie" adopted the "Lead Sled's" tri-color paint scheme, but was painted only blue and gold for subsequent seasons.

The C-121J moves out from NAS Pensacola. When the Tigers arrive at their scheduled show site the Constellation and the maintenance crew will be waiting.

Sixteen thousands horses join the Blue Angel team in 1970 with the arrival of the C-130F.

The biggest Marine on the Blue Angels. His white paint scheme and tail number identify him as the first "Fat Albert."

Tall tails . . . .

1974: A new "Fat Albert" makes his debut over the landscape of north Florida. Still serving on the team today, he makes a colorful impression wherever he goes.

This 1975 shot shows "Albert" with speed brakes, nose gear and main doors extended while the main gear are still recessed.

GySgt. Jessie Wagstaff, flight engineer, at work 19,000 feet above west Texas and two hours away from a landing at NAS El Centro.

A close-up check of the family crest.

Candlestick Park and downtown San Francisco present no traffic jam problems for "Albert."

All aboard for a non-stop coast-to-coast trip with a flight crew of five, a Blue Angel road crew of 25 and 25,000 pounds of equipment.

At most show sites the supply carts are left aboard the transport. However, unloading may be necessary when the C-130F is needed for additional support at an air show.

A six-foot propeller blade is pulled into position. At the end of every flight the props are aligned and intake covers put in place on each engine.

Members of a Navy parachute team drop like snowflakes from a 9' x 10' opening at the rear of "Fat Albert."

Lt. Mike Nord eases the TA-4J into a left wing position. Among its variety of duties the narrator's aircraft serves as a photo platform for aerial shots of the A-4Fs and C-130F.

AME1 Jere Bartz checks over a list of parts and tools unpacked from the C-130F. A counter-check will be made when the equipment is reloaded.

Short field landings may require even a C-130F to deploy a drag chute.

The diamond passes in front of "Albert" as they return from a practice during winter training.

Fat Albert Airlines on another scheduled flight to Anywhere, U.S.A.   Since 1970 the support aircraft has flown the equivalent of 34 trips around the world.

Late night trouble-shooting on a stubborn engine.

On "Fat Albert's" crew deck flight engineer GySgt. Jesse Wagstaff, navigator MGySgt. Tom Asbjornsen and radio operator SSgt. Dale Tinline keeps things running smoothly.

One of "Albert's" pilots, Maj. Chip Perrault, has a balcony seat for a show at NAS Corpus Christi.

A raft is returned to its wing storage compartment following a check of it and other survival gear necessary to over-the-water flights.

The Blue Angels visit the USAF Thunderbirds in 1977 for the teams' annual seminar. "Fat Albert's" presence adds a reminder of the days when the Thunderbirds had their own support aircraft.

A final run-up of the engines followed by a run-down of the last few items on the check list and "Fat Albert" is on his way again.

Putting a gold tip on a silver blade.

Fat Albert Airlines has a unique distinction ... the passengers and luggage all travel in the same compartment.

A peek inside the hangar where those pesky Skyhawks stay.

Flight mechanic SSgt. Herb Vogt listens as a new member of the Blues, AA Ken Jares, asks questions about the C-130F's radar.

A view from the rear of an empty cargo compartment shows the seats which may be lowered and the roller ramps which aid in the loading and unloading of heavy equipment. Above and beyond the forward wall is the flight deck.

At a Florida show site "Fat Albert" and the TA-4J sit in the background as aviation writer Martin Caidin moves his German Ju52 into position for a WWII Warbirds demonstration.

"Fat Albert" and family.

There is never a doubt who crews "Fat Albert."

A panoramic view from the rear seat of #7 includes a belly view of Blue Angel #9.

An impressive background for the walk down.

ALL ROADS LEAD FROM PENSACOLA

Any Blue Angel lives in a world of contrasts -- the humid white beaches of north Florida to the dry, yellow sands of southern California . . .the simple companionship of family at an evening meal to the autographs and handshakes with thousands following an air show - and the quiet of a row of chocked jets along a flight line at sundown to the roar of those same jets thundering into an afternoon sky.

It's a world that produces fatigue, balanced by dedication, practice balanced by perfection and personal sacrifices balanced by pride.

An officer normally spends two years with the team, an enlisted person three to four years. During that time, each person puts in long hours doing the job which is his or her specialty, but also willingly gives additional time whenever or wherever needed to help another teammate.

Since 1955 home has been NAS Pensacola but it has only been a parttime home. As a base for providing needed support facilities and a central location for show deployments, NAS Pensacola is tops. But for daily practice with little interference from either weather or airspace priority requirements, other parts of the country are better suited.

Since 1954 the team has spent 60-70 days annually engaged in winter training far from Pensacola. From 1954-1957 El Centro, California, served as their home away from home. From 1958-1962 Key West, Florida,

had the honors with the Blues switching to NAS Litchfield near Phoenix, Arizona, for 1963-1966.

In 1967 the team returned to NAS El Centro. The base lies in the Imperial Valley of southern California a few miles west of the community from which it gets its name. Thick, green, rectangular fields of lettuce and other produce surround the base but outside any irrigated area the true conditions of the arid scrub brush and cactus of the Mojave desert is clearly evident.

The base has long been the home of the National Parachute Test Range. However, during the past several years much of the base's operation has been moved elsewhere. As a result, the Blue Angels have been left with a quiet, almost excellent condition for practice, practice and more practice.

Pilots, support personnel, the Skyhawk IIs and Fat Albert all arrive in early January. Ahead lie hundreds of hours of flying, talk of flying machines and work on flying machines. During winter training, new team members are just beginning to learn the Blue Angel way of doing things, others are serving their last few months while helping the newcomers adjust, but most are veteran Blues with one or more show seasons behind them and another beginning in mid-March.

Each practice day starts early and ends late. The morning maintenance crew arrives before dawn. Necessary pre-flight activities are attended to in preparation for an 0700 launch. The pilots, also up early, must spend

time in their pre-flight brief before each launch. Several team members drive more than 20 miles into the desert to the team's practice area where they videotape each session.

During the first few weeks of January the diamond will practice separately from the two solo aircraft. In maneuvers, the wingtips will be as much as 15 feet apart and the solos will give each other wide berths as they converge on opposing routines. As the days of practice go by the diamond and solos move their planes closer together and by mid-February the team is flying six-ship formations and honing the timing of each maneuver.

Whether the early morning practice involves four and two aircraft separately or all six jets together, the return of the jets to the ramp signals the start of an ant-like hustle for the ground personnel. As the pilots depart to debrief, the maintenance crew swarms over the A-4Fs. Every surface is inspected, internal lines checked, tanks refueled, tires changed if necessary, parachutes repacked if a chute landing was practiced and any repair attended to whether discovered by an alert crewman or resulting from a returning pilot's complaint of a problem in the air.

While the aircraft are attended to, the administrative jobs of scheduling, reports, public relations preparation and daily coordinated contacts with their counterparts at NAS Pensacola continue.

By late morning another four and two or

six-ship launch has put the planes back into the air over the practice area for a second and last time. On return, debrief includes numerous reruns of the videotapes and the morning crew turns the ground work over to the afternoon crew. Depending upon the requirements of each aircraft, the maintenance crews reenact most of the between launch activities as well as taking care of any newly discovered problems or ones which were not serious enough to be attended to earlier. Some days the team is finished by late afternoon. Often, painting duties or major repairs result in their working late into the evenings. If necessary, they are replaced by a night crew which may find itself still at work as the morning crew returns.

But even El Centro is not all work. The men find time for keeping in physical shape through running, tennis, softball games, etc., and there are many friends from the local community who visit the squadron to talk or bring home-baked goodies. Each year the town of El Centro holds a special banquet for the team they consider to be "their own."

Through the months of training, Fat Albert has been flying weekly round trips between Pensacola and El Centro. In mid-March the Blue Angels pack up their equipment, load Fat Albert for the last time, send all personnel home who are not scheduled to work the first weekend air show, taxi their A-4Fs to the brake release point and head skyward toward their new show season, leaving NAS El Centro behind - until next January.

On return to NAS Pensacola, the team is welcomed home by family, friends and fellow squadron mates. The familiar offices and shop areas in hangar #1853 are again alive with the bustle of everyone shifting to their routine for the busy weeks and months ahead. During winter training only a small force of Blues stays in Florida handling mostly administrative duties, show coordination and Fat Albert's flights, but with everyone home, the offices and shops reflect the sudden influx of people and equipment.

Although they're home, the Blues have little time to enjoy the lush mixed forests, miles of white dune beaches, or crystal-clear, blue-green Gulf waters that surround them on all sides.

The team plans its March through November show season around a repetitious weekly schedule. Mondays through Wednesdays are spend in Pensacola getting ready for the weekend deployment. The planes are attended to by their crews like athletes being readied for the next game. Systems are checked and re-checked, painted surfaces are retouched and any additional maintenance is performed. The team's information officer and his personnel review and finalize the schedule for the next show site and check on the status of various future sites. In conferences, the pilots review all aspects of the past weekend's show and prepare for the next. Practice shows are flown and correspondence is attended to.

On Wednesday the team's narrator and his crew chief depart for the next demonstration site to prepare and coordinate the rest of the team's arrival the following day.

Thursday morning finds the Blue Angels on their way to their next show site. Once there, they will fly their demonstrations and attend to a variety of public appearances and activities. Following their final Sunday show it's back to Pensacola where the routine begins all over again.

A strong reminder of the past stands at the entrance to NAS El Centro.

A tail section of an A-4F is eased out of the hangar. A quick glance ensures the vertical stabilizer will clear the overhang.

Thumbs up signals the proper functioning of all control surfaces of the A-4F.

The left landing gear is lifted clear of the ramp by a hydraulic jack as two of the Blues change a damaged tire.

West of El Centro the diamond pilots practice a four-ship maneuver. On their return to base the two solo aircraft will enter the practice area to perfect their routines.

Following a start of #6 two of the launch crew hustle the starter hose to #5 where Lt. Cmdr. Tucker sits ready to begin his engine run-up.

AE2 Allen Trimble installs a new generator on the lead solo Skyhawk.

Smoke billows behind the six demonstration aircraft as the launch crew moves toward the ramp area beyond the #6 aircraft.

Line chief AMS1 J. V. King has his eyes locked on the #1 jet as he controls all ground activities of the pre-launch operations.

Cmdr. Bill Newman is silhouetted against a bright morning sky as he mounts up to lead the team into its second morning practice.

Advancing with the appearance of some strange insect moving on segmented legs, #1 leads the other Skyhawks into a precision recovery turn.

Opening one of many panels on the #6 jet. Note the lack of shoes which are taboo on the plane's surfaces because of possible scratches and dirt marks.

A freshly painted A-4F external fuel tank is moved outside after being painted.

Easing the J52-P-408 engine onto its track.

The new engine must be joined to the mother ship by a multitude of connections.

One of the planes sits under the drying rays of the desert sun. A paint crew has just finished her new blue coat and will add the identifying gold trim and Blue Angel decal in the next few days.

#7 sits beyond the fold ladders, helmet bags and chocks like a lonely bird waiting for the return of her sisters.

A new maneuver for the 1979 season, the double farvel, is perfected with repeated practice.

"On the dirty roll the plane had a tendency to . . . ." After each flight a quick discussion ensues concerning the possible need of anything from a fine adjustment to major repairs.

The easiest position for the job of removing paint from the gear surface. Note the use of safety equipment for protection from both paint mist and fumes and the high-pitched whine of the scraper brush.

Long shadows and flight jackets are evidence of a cool 0700 walk-down. By the time the pilots return from their first practice the sun will have turned the air above the apron surface into a shimmering mass of heat waves.

The team illustrator, DM1 Lou Humphery, spends part of his time at winter training preparing new parking signs for spaces near the hangar back in Pensacola.

The new Blue Angel narrator, Lt. Jack Ekl, paces the sandy desert practicing his narration while the A-4Fs practice a maneuver overhead.

As the team's narrator, Lt. Ekl will give many orientation rides during the 1979 season. Here the author is returning from a first-hand look at some of the maneuvers performed by the Blues.

Lt. Ross returns his crew's salute as he begins a walk-around before climbing into the #6 jet.

Placing the jets on their launch marks requires a blend of good old pushing and pulling before all wheels rest on their colored chalk "Xs."

The slot A-4F looks a little strange as she sits pulled apart for an engine change.

A close look at the diamond dirty roll shows #7 getting a chance to fly the slot position. On this occasion McDonnell Douglas photographer Harry Gann is in the back seat getting some shots of the view from inside the diamond.

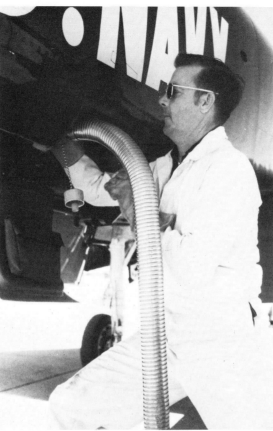

A blue helmet bag containing Lt. Nord's working hat hangs beneath the #3 nose.

Gloves and protective coveralls are donned before the loading of liquid oxygen.

The Blue Angel crest is placed on a Skyhawk II with as much care today as it was on the first jets in 1949.

The solo aircraft have completed their final checks and stand ready to turn onto the active runway as soon as the crewman clears the ramp.

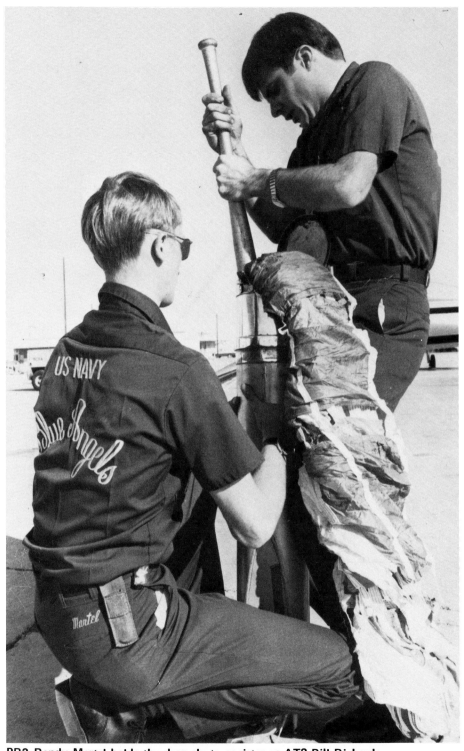

AE1 Ed Johnson gives hand signals to his assistant crew chief and Lt. Tucker as part of the flight control check during launch. Lt. Ross can be seen in the background in #6.

PR2 Randy Martel holds the drag chute canister as AT2 Bill Richards uses a bat to stuff the colorful chute inside.

NAS Pensacola is composed of several smaller fields. This distinctive sign points the way to the field called home by the Blue Angel Squadron.

The Sherman Field section of the base is also home for Squadron VT-4. Some of their aircraft can be seen inside the hangar they share with the Blue Angel squadron.

One of the Blues' former F11A Tigers stands just past the main gate of NAS Pensacola. Another Tiger greets travelers at the city airport.

With memories of glorious days gone by, an F8F Bearcat stands on the grounds of the Naval Museum. The museum, open since 1962, is located near the Blues' hangar. Former Blue Angels Ray Hawkins and Ray Sandelli are on the staff.

"Daddy's home . . . !"

Cmdr. Newman and Lt. Cmdr. Davey enjoy slices of a large cake during
a welcome home party for the team's return from winter training.

144

The show coordinator, YN1 Bob White serves as the Blues' direct contact between each show sponsor and the team.

Lt. Nord loads his briefcase with such items as maps, flight plans, an itinerary and the latest weather data in preparation for a Thursday morning deployment.

Major surgery in progress. It's hard to believe that in a few days she will be back in the skies over Pensacola with her sisters.

A variety of lower floor shops provides everything from tech orders to the smallest nuts and bolts for any maintenance need.

"Fat Albert" moves through the last few miles of airspace toward home. Whether returning from El Centro or the latest show site, the shores of north Florida are always a welcome sight.

Capt. Dan McConnell watches the dials of the C-130F's forward panel as he readies the aircraft for take off.

In the right seat, Capt. Bob Brandon flips a switch as he proceeds through the dozens of items on "Fat Albert's" check list.

A local seamstress, Mrs. Leona Hall, has been the person responsible for the Blues' tailored flight suits since 1972. In this photo the sleeve of Capt. Stankovich's unfinished uniform has the American flag added.

One man in Pensacola has known all the Blue Angels from their beginnings in 1946 to the present. Known affectionately by the name Trader Jon, he is almost as much a legend in Pensacola as the Blues.

The narrator and his crew chief head toward the next show site a day earlier than the rest of the team.

AK2 Bob Cage phones in an order for several A-4F parts as another teammate locates the stock numbers on microfiche.

Capt. Stankovich listens to a discussion of the team's plans for a hospital PR visit at the next show site.

In the upstairs administrative office, YN3 Robin Hohweiler and YN2 Scotty Mayner discuss the processing of temporary duty orders.

Between show weekends #6 is brought inside for some scheduled maintenance.

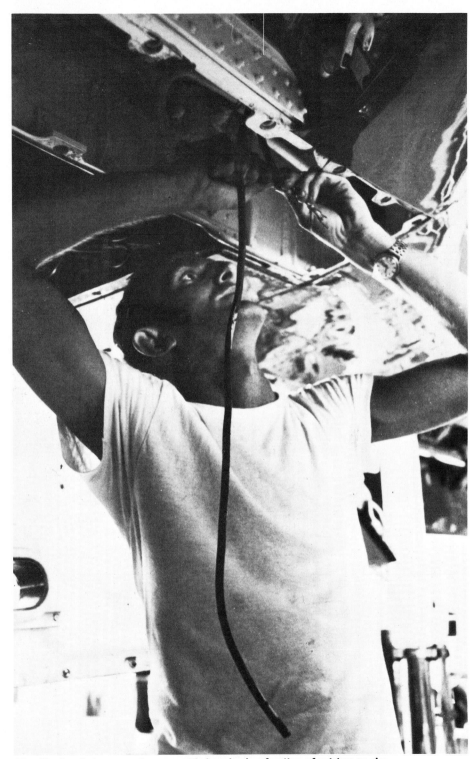

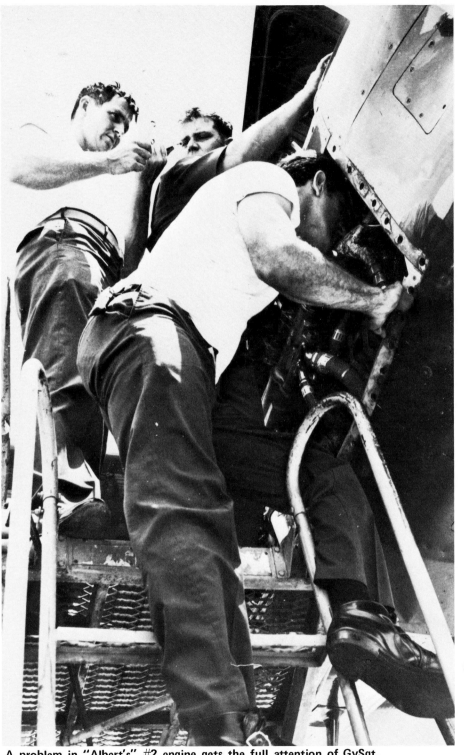

The Skyhawk is a metal maze with hundreds of miles of wiring to the untrained eye. To a specialist like AE1 Red Larson, the repair of a faulty cable is part of any normal day.

A problem in "Albert's" #2 engine gets the full attention of GySgt. Vogt, GySgt. Jim Kreitzer and AD1 Joe Mascaro.

Whether returning from a four-day road trip or a local practice, the ground crew and pilots always practice each recovery as though it was occurring before thousands of spectators.

IMAGES OF BLUE

They started out as five. Now their ranks have grown to more than 160. From an unsure beginning they have become a historic part of Naval aviation. Dressed originally in standard flight suits, brown shoes and soft leather flight caps with goggles, they now wear tailored, colorful flight uniforms, black flight boots and fitted helmets with reflective visors. Their aerial steeds have varied from propeller-driven fighters to the supersonic jets and multiengine transports. Most flew as a part of the demonstration while a smaller number provided support through narration, maintenance or administration. But they are all of one common, elite brotherhood - the Blue Angels.

The competition is keen to make the team. The practice is constant to maintain the team's standards and the spirit is endless even when one's tour is completed.

Not all who were chosen to wear the patch have escaped unharmed. Since 1946, 20 men have lost their lives while performing their duty. But each in his own way helped build the tradition of the Blue Angels. Many are still on active duty status, many have retired, some have served on the team more than once and some have been lost to age or accidents since leaving the team.

Each winter training period brings fresh faces. As always, new people will put on the patch for the first time. They will wear it with pride and they will pass it on with pride - pride in themselves, their mission and the U.S. Navy.

These are the officers of the U.S. Navy Blue Angels.

Cmdr. "Butch" Voris
46-47/52
Leader

Lt. Mel Cassidy
46
Right Wing

Lt. Maurice Wickendoll
46-47
Left Wing/Right Wing

Lt. Al Taddeo
46-47
Left Wing

Lt. (jg) Gale Stouse
46
SNJ

Lt. J. W. Barnitz
46-47
Narrator
Public Affairs Officer

Lt. (jg) Robby Robinson
46
Solo

Lt. Chuck Knight
46-47
Left Wing

Lt. (jg) Billy May
46-48
Right Wing

Lt. Cmdr. Bob Clarke
46-48
Left Wing/Leader

Lt. Bob Thelen
47-48
Slot

Lt. Hal Heagerty
47-49
Right Wing

Lt. Cmdr. "Dusty" Rhodes
47-49
Slot/Leader

Lt. Bob Longworth
48-49
Solo

Lt. Ed Mahood
49
Public Affairs Officer

Lt. George Hoskins
48-50
Right Wing/Slot

Lt. (jg) Fitz Roth
48-50
Left Wing

Lt. Jake Robcke
48-50
Slot

Lt. Cmdr. Johnny Magda
49-50
Leader

Lt. Ralph Hanks
50
Solo

Lt. Bob Belt
49-50/52
Maintenance Officer

Lt. Bud Wood
52
Slot

Lt. Cmdr. Whitey Feightner
52
Solo

Lt. Tom Jones
52
Solo

Lt. Mac MacKnight
48-49/52-53
Right Wing/Solo
Maintenance Officer

Lt. Cmdr. Ray Hawkins
48-50/52-53
Left Wing/Leader

Lt. Cmdr. Frank Graham
49-50/52-53
Narrator

Lt. Pat Murphy
52-53
Right Wing

Lt. Buddy Rich
52-53
Slot/Solo

153

Lt. Auz Aslund
53-54
Left Wing

Lt. Frank Jones
53-54
Solo

Lt. Dayl Crow
53-54
Solo/Right Wing

Capt. Chuck Hiett
54
Solo

Lt. Cmdr. Dick Newhafer
49/54-55
Narrator

Capt. Pete Olson
55
Solo

Capt. Ed Rutty
55
Solo

Cmdr. Zeke Cormier
54-56
Leader

Lt. Ed McKellar
54-56
Solo

Lt. Bill Gureck
55-56
Right Wing/Slot

Lt. (jg) Bob Ittner
55-56
Maintenance Officer

Capt. Chuck Holloway
56
Right Wing

Lt. Cmdr. Harry Sonner
54-57
Maintenance Officer

Lt. Nello Pierozzi
55-57
Left Wing/Right Wing
Slot

Lt. Bruce Bagwell
55-57
Narrator

Lt. Lefty Schwartz
56-57
Solo/Left Wing

1st Lt. Tom Jefferson
57
Solo

Cmdr. Ed Holley
57-58
Leader

Lt. Cmdr. Bill Oleson
57-58
Maintenance Officer

Lt. Mark Perrault
57-59
Public Affairs Officer

Lt. Herb Hunter
57-59
Solo/Left Wing

Lt. Bob Rasmussen
57-59
Right Wing/Slot

Lt. (jg) Gus Kelly
58-59
Maintenance Officer

Capt. Stoney Mayock
58-59
Right Wing

154

Lt. John Damian
58-59
Solo

Lt. Jack Dewenter
58-59
Solo

Lt. Skip Campanella
59
Left Wing

Lt. Don McKee
59
Left Wing

Lt. Bill Sherwood
59
Narrator

Lt. Chuck Elliott
60
Solo

Lt. John Rademacher
60
Solo

Lt. Cmdr. Jack Reavis
58-61
Maintenance Officer

Cmdr. Zeb Knott
59-61
Leader

Lt. Duke Ventigmiglia
60-61
Narrator

Lt. Bill Rennie
60-61
Left Wing

Capt. Doug McCaughey
60-62
Right Wing

Lt. Hank Giedzinski
61-62
Narrator

Lt. Ray Atherton
61-62
Maintenance Officer

Lt. Lew Chatham
61-63
Solo

Lt. Dan MacIntyre
61-63
Solo/Right Wing

Lt. George Neale
62-64
Left Wing/Slot

Lt. Dick Langford
62-64
Solo/Left Wing

Capt. John Kretsinger
63-64
Solo

Lt. Cmdr. Bob Cowles
63-65
Public Affairs Officer

Lt. Cmdr. Scott Ross
63-65
Maintenance Officer

Lt. Bob McDonough
64-65
Right Wing

Lt. Cmdr. Dick Oliver
64-66
Solo

Lt. Frank Mezzadri
64-66
Slot

Cmdr. Bob Aumack
64-66
Leader

Lt. Mike Van Ort
66
Solo

Capt. Fred Craig
65-67
Solo/Right Wing

Lt. Red Hubbard
65-67
Left Wing/Slot

Lt. Cmdr. Jack Cougar
66-67
Maintenance Officer

Lt. Dave Rottgering
66-67
Public Affairs Officer

Lt. Norm Gandia
66-67
Solo

Lt. Frank Gallagher
67
Solo

Capt. Ron Thompson
67
Solo

Lt. Fred Wilson
66-68
Public Affairs Officer

Lt. Hal Loney
67-68
Solo

Lt. Bill Worley
68
Solo

Lt. Smokey Tolbert
68
Solo

Capt. Vince Donile
67-69
Right Wing

Lt. John Allen
67-69
Left Wing/Slot/Solo

Cmdr. Bill Wheat
67-69
Leader

Cmdr. Bud Jourden
68-69
Maintenance Officer

Lt. Rick Millson
68-69
Left Wing/Slot

Lt. Rick Adams
68-69
Narrator

Lt. Ernie Christensen
69-70
Left Wing/Slot

Lt. Steve Shoemaker
69-70
Solo

Lt. Mary Russell
69-70
Administrative Officer

Lt. Dick Schram
69-71
Public Affairs Officer

Lt. Cmdr. Mac Prose
70-71
Maintenance Officer

Lt. Jim Maslowski
70-71
Left Wing/Slot

Capt. Kevin O'Mara
70-71
Right Wing

Lt. Cmdr. J. D. Davis
70-71
Narrator

Cmdr. Harley Hall
70-71
Leader

Lt. Bill Switzer
71-72
Solo/Slot

Lt. Bill Beardsley
71-72
Left Wing

Lt. Larry Watters
72
Narrator

Lt. Gary Smith
72
Narrator

Lt. Cmdr. Don Bently
72-73
Leader

Capt. Mike Murphy
72-73
Right Wing/Slot

Lt. Steve Lambert
72-73
Solo

Lt. Cmdr. Skip Umstead
70-73
Solo/Leader

Lt. Chuck Newcomb
72-74
Public Affairs Officer

Lt. Cmdr. Fred Wiggins
72-74
Maintenance Officer

Capt. John Fogg
73-74
Left Wing/Slot

Lt. Cmdr. Marlin Wiita
73-74
Right Wing

Capt. Ken Wallace
54-55/61-63/74
Slot/Leader
Program Manager

1st Lt. Joe Rodgers
74
Transport Pilot

Capt. Al Coley
74
Transport Pilot

Maj. Don Stiegman
74
Transport Pilot

CWO-2 Clinton Swartz
73-75
Supply Officer

Lt. John Chehansky
73-75
Narrator/Left Wing/Slot

Cmdr. Tony Less
74-75
Leader

Capt. Ron Fleming
74-75
Transport Pilot

Lt. Cmdr. Bob Randolph
74-75
Flight Surgeon

Lt. John Patton
74-76
Narrator/Left Wing/Slot

Lt. Mike Deeter
74-76
Maintenance Officer

Lt. Denny Sapp
75-76
Solo

Capt. Bill Holverstott
75-76
Right Wing

Lt. Nile Kraft
76
Narrator

Lt. Leo Boor
74-77
Administrative Officer

Lt. Jim Bauer
75-77
Events Coordinator
Administrative Officer

Lt. Al Cisneros
75-77
Narrator/Left Wing/Slot

Lt. Cmdr. Vance Parker
74-75/77
Solo

Capt. Steve Petit
75-77
Transport Pilot

Lt. Cmdr. Tim Peterson
75-77
Flight Surgeon

Lt. (jg) Al Pulley
75-77
Supply Officer

Cmdr. Casey Jones
76-77
Leader

Lt. Cmdr. John Miller
76-78
Solo

Maj. Steve Murray
76-78
Transport Pilot

Capt. Phil Brooks
76-78
Transport Pilot

Lt. Ray Sandelli
77-78
Events Coordinator

Lt. Cmdr. Don Simmons
77-78
Left Wing/Slot

Capt. Dan Keating
77-78
Right Wing

Lt. Jack Johnson
77-78
Maintenance Officer

Lt. Bernard Gipson
77-78
Flight Surgeon

Lt. (jg) Robert Faulk
77-78
Supply Officer

Lt. Mike Curtin
78
Solo

Lt. Cmdr. Bill Clark
77-present
Adminstrative Officer

Lt. Cmdr. Bruce Davey
77-79
Narrator/Left Wing/Slot

Lt. Dennis Shafer
78-79
Supply Officer

Cmdr. Bill Newman
78-79
Leader

Lt. Cmdr. Mike Nord
78-present
Narrator/Left Wing/Slot

Capt. Bob Brandon
78-79
Transport Pilot

Capt. Dan McConnell
78-present
Transport Pilot

Lt. Cmdr. Jerry Tucker
73-74/79
Solo

Capt. Fred Stankovich
79-present
Right Wing

Lt. Jim Ross
79-present
Solo

Lt. Cmdr. Jack Ekl
79-present
Narrator/Solo

Lt. Kent Horne
79-present
Events Coordinator

Lt. Cmdr. Ben Woods
79-present
Maintenance Officer

Maj. Chip Perrault
79-present
Transport Pilot

Lt. Cmdr.
Charles Thomason
79-present
Flight Surgeon

Cmdr. Denny Wisely
present
Leader

Lt. Cmdr. Jim Horsley
present
Left Wing

Lt. Randy Clark
present
Narrator

Maj. Ken Hines
present
Transport Pilot

Photos unavailable for the following Blue Angels:

Lt. Ed Oliphant	Maj. Lynn Jackson	Lt. Red Riedl
49-50	54	55
Public Affairs Officer	Transport Pilot	Public Affairs Officer

Cmdr. R. E. Luehrs
55-57
Flight Surgeon

Cmdr. Nick Glasgow
58
Leader

Carol Knotts was born in Georgia in 1941. The daughter of Air Force parents, she has lived in various parts of the United States and overseas. After receiving her BS and MS degrees in Zoology from Northwestern State University in Louisiana, she moved to Bossier City, Louisiana. An instructor at Bossier Parish Community College for the past 12 years, she teaches in the Science Department.

Her interest in aviation developed at an early age and led to publication of her first book in 1978, "Diamond in the Sky," a pictorial account of the U.S. Air Force Thunderbirds. "Reflections of Blue" is the result of her passion for flight — especially in the areas of aerial demonstration teams and World War II aircraft.

Also by Carol Knotts

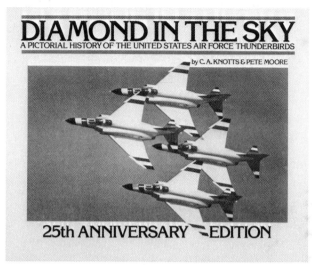

DIAMOND IN THE SKY
A PICTORIAL HISTORY OF THE UNITED STATES AIR FORCE THUNDERBIRDS
by C.A. KNOTTS & PETE MOORE

25th ANNIVERSARY EDITION

Thunderbirds! One of the world's premier military aerobatic teams. Now their complete history is in an exciting new book! Over five hundred photos detail the teams' complete history from the earliest days of the Thunderjet to the current era of T-38's.

Formation flying, precision maneuvers, wing-tip to wing-tip aerobatics, dramatic photos, the men, machines, practice sessions, airshows, maintenance, photos from inside aircraft during aerobatics, support equipment, paint schemes, personal markings, famous personalities, "incidents" and problems; they're all included.

Each aircraft type used by the team is detailed in a complete chapter. Included are specifications, modifications, paint schemes, and performance characteristics. Coverage includes F-4 Phantom, Thunderjet, F-84 Thunderstreak, F-100 Super Sabre, F-105 Thunderchief, T-38, and more!

The book is 11" × 9" in size, softbound, and contains 168 pages with a full color section covering each aircraft type used by the team.

Available from your bookseller or direct from the publisher.